he knows how you feel

Sister Jean Marie, O.S.B.

A Benedictine Sister of Perpetual Adoration

Published by
Liguorian Pamphlets & Books
Liguori, Missouri 63057

Imprimi Potest:
   Daniel L. Lowery, C.SS.R.
   Provincial, St. Louis Province
   Redemptorist Fathers
   March 22, 1971

Imprimatur:
   St. Louis, March 25, 1971
   + George J. Gottwald
   Vicar General of St. Louis

With love and gratitude, this book is dedicated
to Brother Ron . . . a man who knows how it feels . . .

*. . . ours were the sufferings he
bore . . . ours the sorrows he
carried.*

(Is. 53:4)

PHOTO CREDITS:

Anheuser Busch, Inc.

Herbert Keppler

Religious News Service

St. Louis Review (Richard Finke et al)

Sister M. Reparata , o.s.b.

We are deeply grateful to all who, through their generosity, made this publication possible by helping us to secure "just the right photographs."

INTRODUCTION

Sometimes we feel so desperately alone in our sufferings. It helps when we know that someone feels with us, that someone understands. Even our joys are short-lived, unless they are shared with others and are felt in some way by them.

Ordinarily, we seek consolation in our sorrows and share our joys with immediate friends. They look on us as persons, not as objects and because of this they truly know how we feel. They cry with us and laugh with us, just as we cry and laugh with them. When there is no occasion for laughter or tears or even conversation, they are there offering their companionship. Their mere presence is often the greatest sign of love and friendship.

Our true friends know how we feel because they love us. They identify with us so completely that our thoughts and sentiments become their thoughts and sentiments.

The love which springs from their openness to us and our openness to them is more than chemical reaction. It is the result of that spiritual reality we call "being Christian." At Baptism, God's love was "poured into our hearts through the Holy Spirit" (Rom. 5:5). We became saturated, soaked through and through, with divine love. And the only way we can dry up His love is to expose ourselves rashly to the sunburn of sin. When we return God's love, we are loving God in us, which is the reason for and the meaning of love for self.

We cannot love others unless we love ourselves first of all. Of ourselves we do not have enough human love to fulfill us and others. We bathe in God's love and since it is so abundant we share it with others.

And that is what this book is all about. It is a reminder that Christ, the God-man abides in every Christian. It prompts us to reflect that Christ in His human nature experienced the joys and sorrows of mankind. Because He was God He could not sin. But He accepted the burden of our sins, and in doing so He endured sorrow beyond our comprehension.

Yes, Christ knows how it feels.

Christopher Farrell, C.SS.R.
Editor, Liguorian Books

Do you know how it feels?...

To enjoy a quiet walk in a quiet place . . .

Sister M. Reparata, o.s.b.

To be safe and secure . . .

To be united with your brothers in a cause . . .

He called the Twelve together and gave them power and authority ... and He sent them out to proclaim the kingdom of God and to heal.

Luke 9:1

To be at war . . .

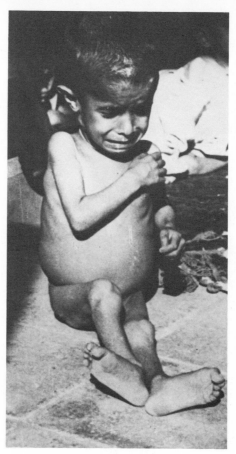

To be hungry . . .

He fasted for forty days and forty nights.

Matthew 4:2

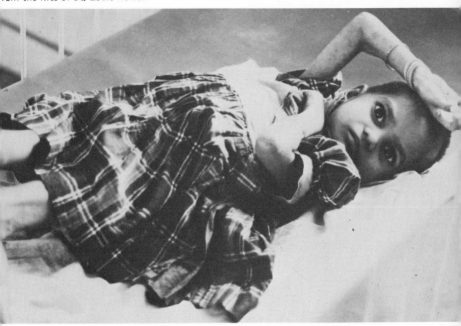

And weak . . .

To be old and alone . . .

To have problems that seem to have no solution . . .

To lose all you have . . .

For Him I have accepted the loss of everything, and I look on everything as so much rubbish if only I can have Christ and be given a place in Him.

To feel that the world is crumbling
about you . . .

Religious News Service

To be worn out from worry . . .

And, yet, to hope . . .

We must hope to be saved since we are not saved yet – it is something we must wait for with patience.

Romans 8:25

21

To enjoy the ocean, the shore, the salt air, the sound of the surf, the warmth of the sun . . .

To wonder . . .

To be fenced-in

or kept out . . .

Religious News Service

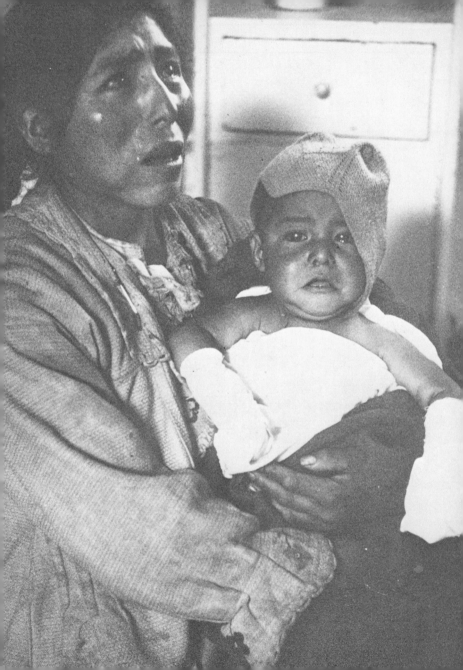

To plead . . .

'My Father,' He said *'if this cup cannot pass by without My drinking it, Your will be done!'*

Matthew 26:42

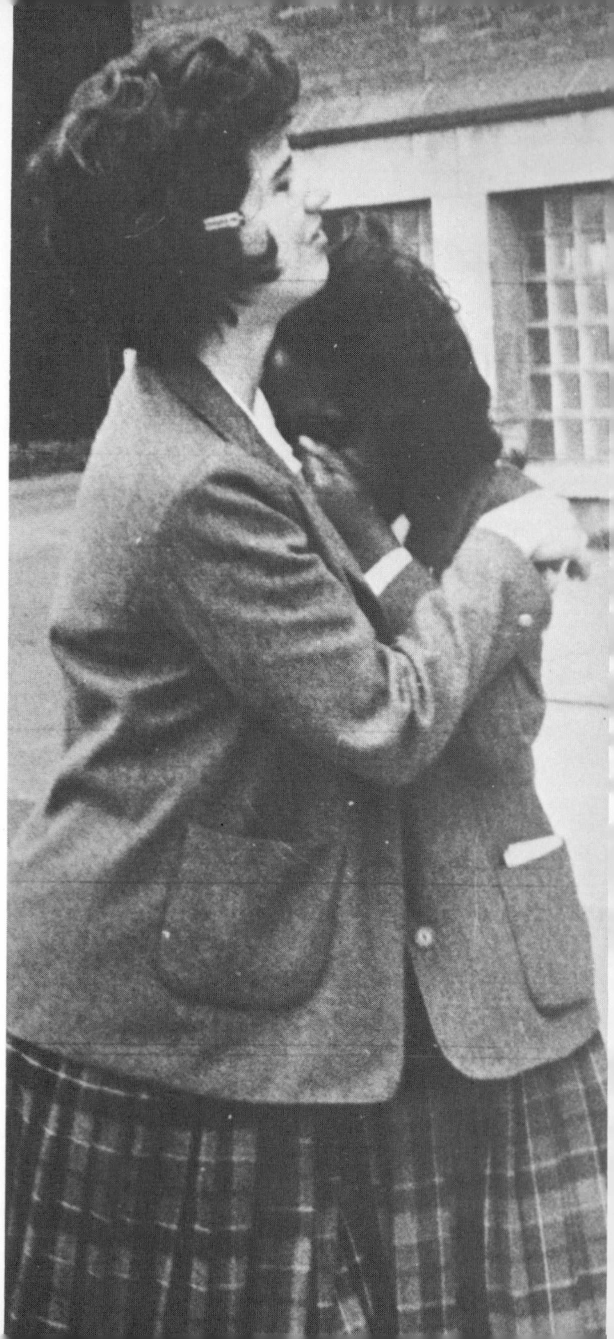

Religious News Service

To be grief-stricken . . .

At the sight of her tears . . . Jesus said in great distress, with a sigh that came straight from the heart, 'Where have you put him?' . . . Jesus wept; and the Jews said, 'See how much He loved him!'

John 11:33-37

To be wary . . .

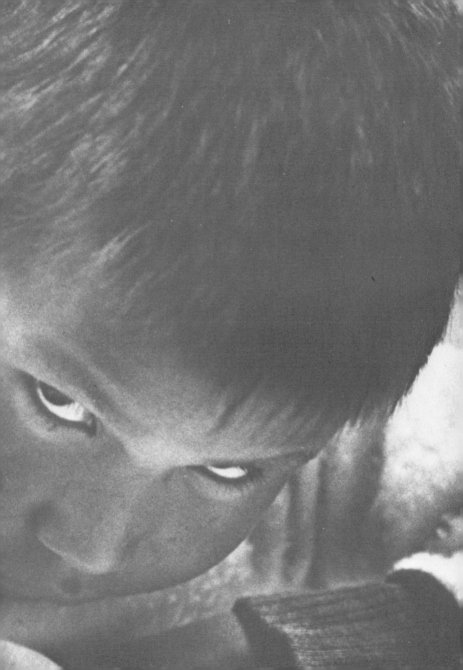

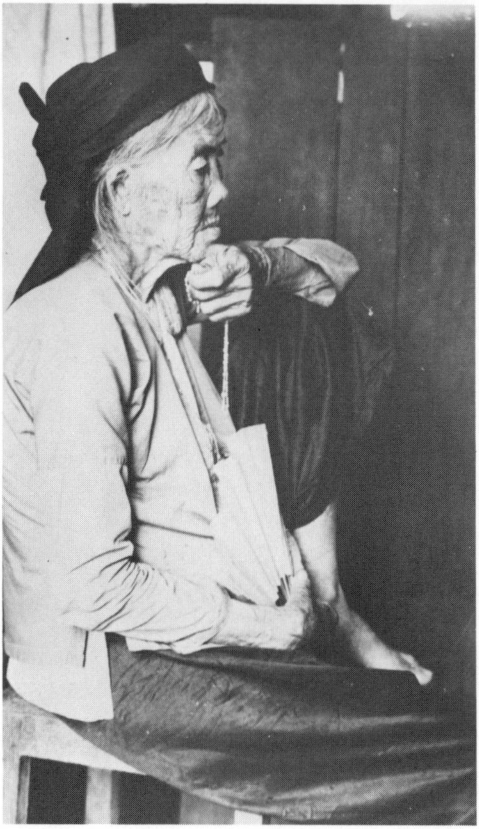

from the files of St. Louis Review

To wait . . .

Then He told them a parable about the need to pray continually and never lose heart.

Luke 18:1

To be a little "off-center" (sometimes)
when things pile up . . . one snowflake
too many . . .

Richard Finke

To be respected by your friends . . .

It can only be to God's glory, then, for you to treat each other in the same friendly way as Christ treated you.

Romans 15:7

To bear the burden
of responsibility . . .

You should carry each other's troubles and fulfill the law of Christ. It is the people who are not important who often make the mistake of thinking that they are.

Galatians 6:2-3

To buckle down and be serious sometimes . . .

To tackle a guy who's bigger 'n you are . . .

To have faith when all odds
are against you . . .

*Jesus answered them: ' . . . In the world you will have trouble,
but be brave:*
I have conquered the world.'

from the files of St. Louis Review

To see in a bit of "nature" a reminder
of redemption . . .

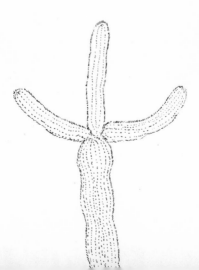

To get together with your friends and
talk about things that matter . . .

Richard Finke

And from early morning the people would gather
round Him in the Temple to listen to Him.

Luke 21:38

To lose something and have friends who help you search . . .

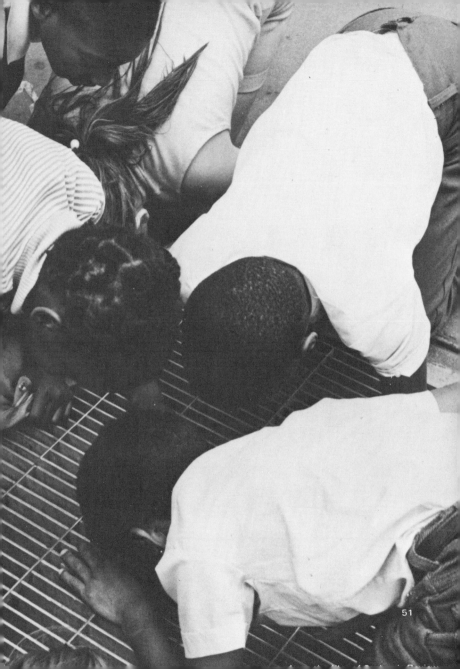

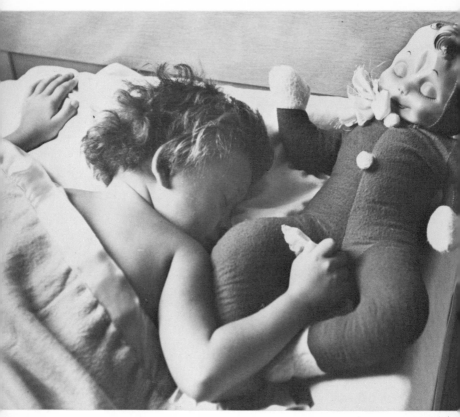

from the files of St. Louis Review

To sleep peacefully . . .

So they put to sea, and as they sailed He fell asleep.
Luke 8:23

from the files of St. Louis Review

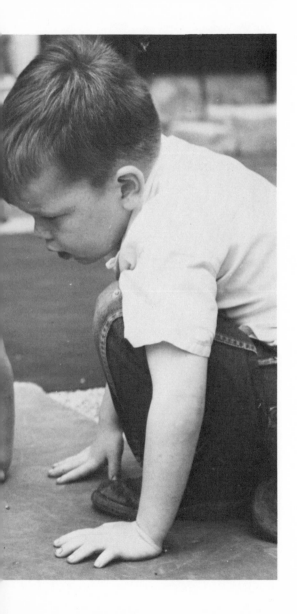

To be
fascinated . . .

To love and be loved . . .

Love one another;
just as I have loved you,
you also must love one another.

John 13:34

To be comforted . . .

Happy those who mourn: they shall be comforted.
Matthew 5:5

To be treated like a person . . .

If I, then, the Lord and Master, have washed your feet, you should wash each other's feet.

John 13:14

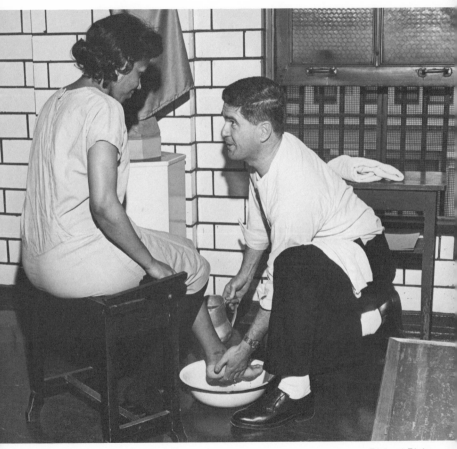

Richard Finke

61

To come to grips with a burden too heavy to carry alone . . .

As they were leading Him away they seized on a man, Simon from Cyrene . . . and made him shoulder the cross and carry it behind Jesus.

To be out early on a crisp morning . . . when everything seems so "new" and fresh . . .

To contribute . . . to do your share . . .

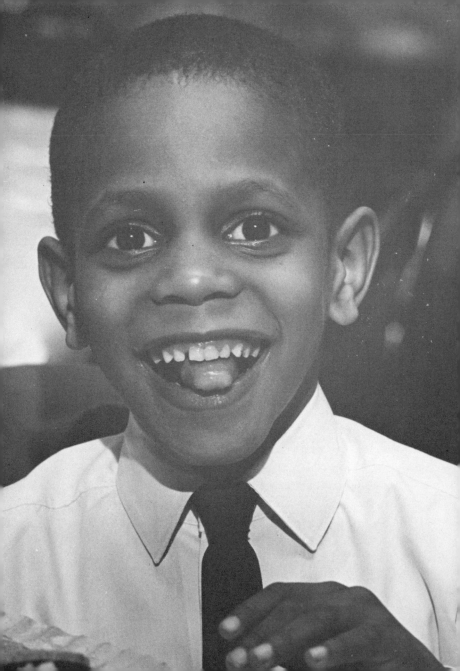

To be delighted . . .

If you keep My commandments
you will remain in My love . . .
I have told you this
so that My own joy may be in you
and your joy be complete.

John 15:10-11

To be bewildered . . . to try hard to understand . . .

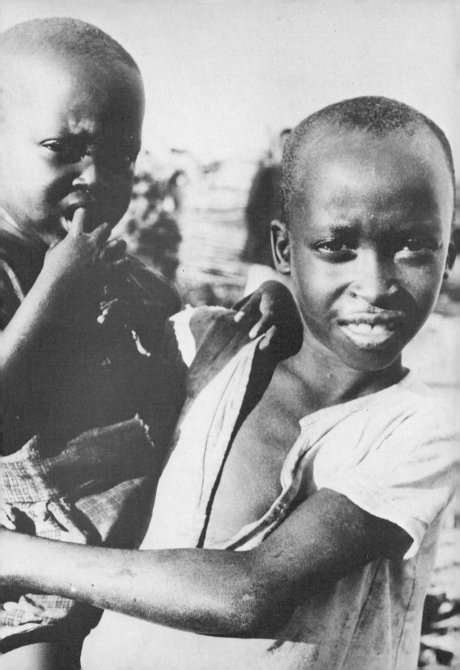

Richard Finke

To look forward to
happy holidays . . .

To absorb the stillness of the desert . . .

So Jesus . . . left the district for a town called Ephraim, in the country bordering on the desert, and stayed there with His disciples.

John 11:53-54

To have a friend who likes the things you like . . .

Anheuser Busch, Inc.

To go off by yourself sometimes . . .

His reputation continued to grow, and large crowds would gather to hear Him and to have their sickness cured, but He would always go off to some place where He could be alone and pray.

Luke 5:15-16

And to be "one of the gang" . . .

There was a wedding at Cana in Galilee. The mother of Jesus was there, and Jesus and His disciples had also been invited.

John 2:1

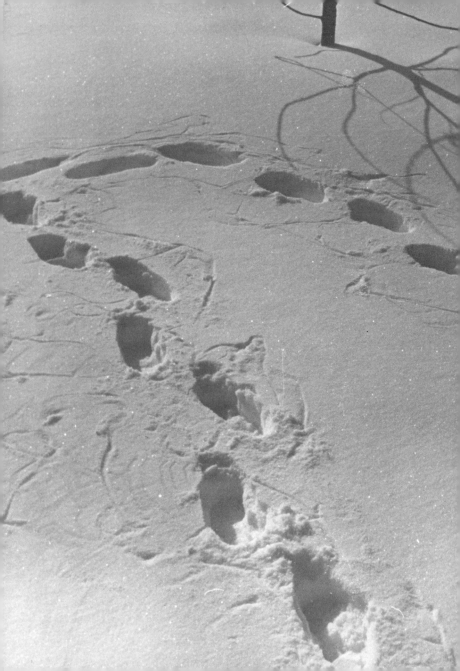

Sister M. Reparata, o.s.b.

To wonder
(sometimes)
if you're
coming
or going . . .

To be pleased with yourself . . .

To see and
appreciate beauty . . .

Sister M. Reparata, o.s.b.

I know how it feels. I've felt the things you feel . . . enjoyed the things you enjoy . . . I know what it's like to be human.

YOU are My body. I could not possibly be unaware or indifferent to anything that affects you. But . . . even more than that . . . I count on you to be My hands . . . reaching out to comfort one . . . or folded in prayer for many. Through *you* I am incarnate at this moment in time . . . in this culture.

I am a *living* God . . . and *relevant*! I want you to know Me very well . . . No cold handshakes . . . only warm embraces. It's love that I want . . . do you know how that feels?

The Word was made flesh,
He lived among us,
And we saw His glory,
the glory that is His as the only Son of the Father,
full of grace and truth.

John 1:14